Introduction

If you've recently learned to knit (whether someone taught you, you took a class, or you taught yourself online), here comes the hard part.

You feel you know the basics, and you're sure you can manipulate those two sticks and create something wonderful, but the patterns you find online or in magazines seem too difficult. Meanwhile the easy patterns look like they'd produce the most ugly results.

Well, welcome to the answer to your problem!

Collected in this book are the kinds of patterns that we used in our early knitting days. Here you'll find patterns for projects that we enjoyed making and projects that we enjoyed using or were happy to give as gifts.

But most important: all of the patterns are intended for beginners just like you.

So join us for a walk through the pages of this book. Select a hat that changes styles with a mere flick of the border, afghans to keep you warm, a scarf that makes you think you are wearing fur, a bag for carrying all of your knitting gear that is made with yarn that creates—as if by magic—stripes, and much more.

And although this book is geared toward beginners, an advanced knitter may very well find it impossible to resist knitting some of the fantastic items included here.

Can't remember exactly what you once learned? Confused as to what those abbreviations and symbols mean? Spend a little time with our Stitch Guide and Special Helps on pages 47 and 48. Here we've given you an in-depth explanation of how to work all of the stitches we've used in these patterns.

So choose a pattern, settle down with a cup of tea, a pair of knitting needles, some great yarn, and let the new world of knitting open up for you.

You'll be glad you did.

Magical Hat

Designed by Nazanin S. Fard for Red Heart®

Imagine a very simple to make hat that turns into another style completely with a flip of the cuff. Wear it with the cuff flipped up, or turn it into a slouchy hat with the cuff turned down.

Beginner-Friendly Knitting

by Rita Weiss

Leisure Arts, Inc.
Maumelle, Arkansas

Produced by

Production Team

Creative Directors: Jean Leinhauser and Rita Weiss

Pattern Testers: Kimberly Britt

Patricia Honaker

Book Design: Linda Causee

Diagrams © 2015 by The Creative Partners™LLC

Reproduced by special permission

We have made every effort to ensure that these instructions are accurate and complete. We cannot, however, be responsible for human error, typographical mistakes or variations in individual work

Published by Leisure Arts, Inc.

© 2015 by Leisure Arts, Inc.

104 Champs Boulevard, Ste. 100

Maumelle, AR 72113-6738

www. leisurearts.com

ISBN-13: 978-1-4647-3370-3

SKILL LEVEL

Easy

FINISHED SIZE

Fits 20" (51 cm) head circumference

MATERIALS

Worsted weight yarn
[59% acrylic, 18% polyester, 15% metallic, 8% wool, 3.5 ounces, 190 yards (100 grams, 174 meters) per skein]

 1 skein multi-colored

Note: *Photographed model made with Red Heart® Boutique Magical™ #1406 Hocus Pocus*
Size 8 (5 mm) knitting needles (or size required for gauge)
Yarn needle

GAUGE

16 stitches = 4" (10.16 cm) in pattern

STITCH GUIDE

K: knit

P: purl

YO: yarn over a needle; creates one stitch

K2tog: knit 2 stitches together; decreases one stitch

P2tog: purl 2 stitches together; decreases one stitch

INSTRUCTIONS

Starting at the bottom of the hat, cast on 87 stitches loosely.

Row 1 (right side): K1; *P2, K2; repeat from * across the row, ending with P2.

Row 2: *K2, P2; repeat from * across to the last 3 stitches, K2, P1.

Repeat Rows 1 and 2 until the piece measures 10" from the cast on row, ending by working a wrong side row.

Shaping the Top

Row 1: K1; *P2, K2tog; repeat from * across, ending with P2: 66 stitches.

Row 2: *K2, P1; repeat from * across to the last stitch, P1.

Row 3: K1; *P2tog, K1; repeat from * across, ending with P2tog: 44 stitches.

Row 4: *K1, P1; repeat from * across.

Row 5: *K2tog; repeat from * across: 22 stitches.

Row 6: K1, purl to last stitch, K1.

Row 7: K1; *K2tog; repeat from * to last stitch, K1: 12 stitches.

Row 8: K1, purl to last stitch, K1.

Cut the yarn, leaving a long end. Thread the yarn into yarn needle and draw the end through the remaining stitches and pull the yarn tightly. Use the thread to sew the center back seam.

Plum Ripple

Sweet as a taste of a delicious plum, this pretty rosy ripple will show off your knitting skills.

SKILL LEVEL

Easy

FINISHED SIZE

Approx 48" x 64" (121.92 cm x 162.56 cm)

MATERIALS

Worsted weight yarn

[100% acrylic, 5 ounces, 230 yards (141 grams, 211 meters) per skein]

8 skeins multi-color

Note: *Photographed model made with Red Heart® With Love® #1942 Plum Jam*

36" Size 9 (5.5 mm) circular knitting needle (or size required for gauge)

GAUGE

19 stitches = 4" (10.16 cm) in pattern

STITCH GUIDE

K: knit

K2 tog: knit 2 stitches together; decreases one stitch

YO: yarn over a needle; creates one stitch

INSTRUCTIONS

Cast on 234 stitches.

Note: *Do not join; work back and forth in rows.*

First Border

Rows 1 through 5: Knit across.

Main Section

Row 1 (right side): Knit across.

Row 2: Purl across.

Row 3: (K2tog) 3 times; *(YO, K1) 6 times, (K2tog) 6 times; repeat from * to last 12 stitches; (YO, K1) 6 times, (K2tog) 3 times.

Row 4: Knit.

Repeat Rows 1 through 4 until afghan measures about 61" from the cast on row, ending by working a Row 3.

Second Border

Rows 1 through 4: Knit across.

Finish off.

Pretty Pot Holder

Create more cheer in the kitchen with this useful and attractive pot holder.

SKILL LEVEL

Easy

FINISHED SIZE

Approx: 8" x 8" (20.32 cm x 20.32 cm)

MATERIALS

Worsted weight cotton yarn

[100% combed cotton, 2 ounces, 98 yards
(56. 7 grams, 89.6 meters) per ball]

    2 balls green stripes

Note: *Photographed model made with Red Heart®
Creme de la Creme® #965 Greentones.*

Size 7 (4.5 mm) straight knitting needles (or size
required for gauge)

Two Size 7 (4.5 mm) double-pointed knitting needles

GAUGE

15 stitches = 2" (5.08 cm) in pattern

STITCH GUIDE

K: knit

Sl: slip the stitch from one needle to the next
without working it

P: purl

INSTRUCTIONS

Note: *All slip stitches are worked as if to purl.*

Starting at the bottom of the pot holder, cast on 60
stitches.

Rows 1 and 2: *K1, sl 1, P1, sl 1; repeat from * across.

Rows 3 and 4: *P1, sl 1, K1, sl 1; repeat from * across.

Repeat Rows 1 through 4 until pot holder measures
8" (20.32 cm). Bind off 58 stitches, leaving 3 stitches
on the needle. Place the 3 stitches on one double-
pointed needle and work the hanging cord. The cord
is worked from the right side only; do not turn.

Row 1: With a second double-pointed needle, K2.
Do not turn. Slide the stitches to the opposite end of
the needle.

Row 2: Take the yarn around the back side of the
stitches and with first needle, K3; do not turn. Slide
stitches to the opposite side of the needle.

Repeat Rows 1 and 2 until the cord is approximately
3" (7.62 cm). Finish off by knitting 3 stitches together,
and sew the loose end of the hanging cord to the
pot holder to make a loop.

Colorful Leg Warmers

Keep warm while dreaming of being a prima ballerina.

SKILL LEVEL

Easy

FINISHED SIZE

For adult: approx 24" long x 10¾" wide at top (60.96 cm x 27.31 cm)

MATERIALS

Worsted weight yarn 4

[100% acrylic, 5 ounces, 236 yards (141 grams, 215 meters) per skein]

    1 skein multi-color (A)

[100% acrylic, 7 ounces, 364 yards (198 grams, 333 meters per skein]

    1 skein yellow (B)

    1 skein green (C)

    1 skein red (D)

Note: *Photographed model made with Red Heart® Super Saver® #3934 Day Glow (A), #324 Bright Yellow (B), #672 Spring Green (C) and #390 Hot Red (D).*

Sizes 7 (4.5 mm), 8 (5 mm), 10 (6 mm), 10½ (6.5 mm) knitting needles (or size required for gauge)

Yarn needle

GAUGES

In stockinette stitch (knit one row, purl one row):

With size 7 needles, 20 sts = 4" (10.16 cm)

With size 8 needles, 18 sts = 4" (10.16 cm)

With size 10 needles, 16 sts = 4" (10.16 cm)

With size 10½ needles, 15 sts = 4" (10.16 cm)

STITCH GUIDE

K: knit

P: purl

INSTRUCTIONS (make 2)

1. With A (multi-color yarn) and the size 7 needles, cast on 40 sts. Work in a ribbing (K1, P1) for 3" (7.62 cm). Cut A and attach B (yellow yarn).

2. With B (yellow yarn) and size 7 needles, work in stockinette stitch (knit 1 row, purl 1 row) for 3" (7.62 cm). Cut B and attach C (green yarn).

3. Change to size 8 needles and work in stockinette stitch for 3" (7.62 cm) with C. Cut C (green yarn) and attach D (red yarn). Work in stockinette stitch for 2" (5.08 cm) with D (red yarn).

4. Change to size 10 needles and work 1" (2.54 cm) more in stockinette stitch with D (red yarn). Cut D (red yarn) and attach A (multi-color yarn). Knit 3" (7.62 cm) in stockinette stitch with A (multi-color yarn). Cut A (multi-color yarn) and attach B (yellow yarn). Knit 2" (5.08 cm) in stockinette stitch with B (yellow yarn).

5. Change to size 10½ needles and work 1" (2.54 cm) more in stockinette stitch with B (yellow yarn). Cut B (yellow yarn) and attach C (green yarn). Work 3" (7.62 cm) in stockinette stitch with C (green yarn). Cut C (green yarn) and attach D (red yarn).

6. With D (red yarn) and 10½ needles, work in a ribbing (K1, P1) for 3" (7.62 cm). Finish off very loosely in ribbing. Sew the side seam neatly. Weave in all ends.

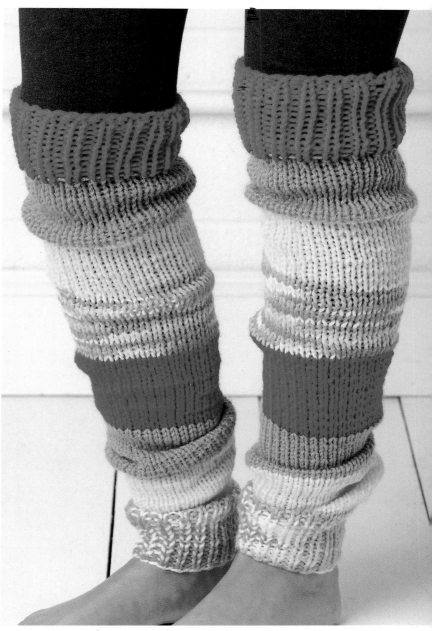

Everybody's Favorite Hat

Designed by Cathy Payson for Red Heart®

The perfect hat that will look great on everyone, any a guy or a gal.

SKILL LEVEL

Easy

FINISHED SIZE

Approx 20" (50.8 cm) circumference, unstretched

Hat will stretch to fit 21" to 22" (53.34 cm to 55.88 cm) head

MATERIALS

Bulky weight yarn

[80% acrylic, 20% wool, 3.5 ounces, 106 yards (100 grams, 97 meters) per skein]

    1 ball blue (A)

    1 ball orange (B)

Note: *Photographed model made with Red Heart® Heads Up #872 Royale (A) and #262 Tangelo (B)*

Size 10½ (6.5 mm) knitting needles (or size required for gauge)

Yarn needle

GAUGE

11 sts = 4" (10.16 cm) in garter stitch (knit each row)

STITCH GUIDE

K: knit

K2tog: knit 2 stitches together; decreases one stitch

INSTRUCTIONS

With A, cast on 55 stitches.

Row 1 (wrong side): Knit across. Change to B.

Row 2: With B, knit across.

Row 3: With B, knit across.

Row 4: With B, knit across.

Row 5: With B, knit across. Change to A.

Row 6: With A, knit across.

Row 7: With A, knit across.

Rows 8 through 11: Repeat Rows 2, 3, 4 and 5.

At the end of Row 11, cut B, and work remainder of hat with A only.

Knit every row until the piece measures 5" (12.7 cm), ending with a wrong side row.

Crown (top of hat)

Row 1 (right side): *K9, K2tog; repeat from * across: 50 stitches.

Row 2: Knit across.

Row 3: *K8, K2tog; repeat from * across: 45 stitches.

Row 4: Knit across.

Row 5: *K7, K2tog; repeat from * across: 40 stitches.

Row 6: Knit across.

Row 7: *K6, K2tog; repeat from * across: 35 stitches.

Row 8: Knit across.

Row 9: *K5, K2tog; repeat from * across: 30 stitches.

Row 10: Knit across.

Row 11: *K4, K2tog; repeat from * across: 25 stitches.

Row 12: Knit across.

Row 13: *K3, K2tog; repeat from * across: 20 stitches.

Row 14: Knit across.

Row 15: *K2, K2tog; repeat from * across: 15 stitches.

Row 16: Knit across.

Row 17: *K1, K2tog; repeat from * across: 10 stitches.

Row 18: Knit across.

Row 19: *K2tog; repeat from * across: 5 stitches.

Row 20: *Knit across.

Cut A, leaving a long tail. Thread the tail through the remaining 5 stitches and remove them from the needle. Pull to gather. Sew the side edges together for the back seam.

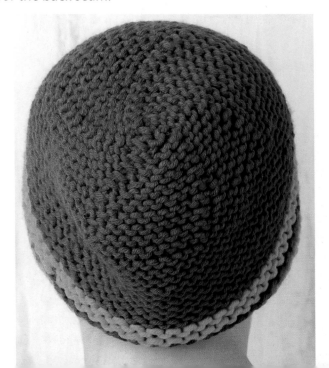

Elegance with Warmth

Fun and easy to make, the hat and scarf will be an excellent addition to anyone's wardrobe.

SKILL LEVEL

Easy

FINISHED SIZE

Scarf: Approx 7" x 72" (17.78 cm x 182.88 cm)

Hat: Fits up to 22" (55.88 cm) head

MATERIALS

Worsted weight yarn 【4】

[100% acrylic, 7 ounces, 370 yards (198 grams, 338 meters) per skein]

    1 skein purple (A)

    1 skein white (B)

Note: *Photographed model made with Red Heart ® With Love® #1542 Aubergine and #1303 Aran.*

Size 7 (4.5 mm) knitting needles (or size required for gauge)

GAUGE

10 sts=2" (5.08 cm) in garter stitch (knit each row)

STITCH GUIDE

K: knit

K2tog: Knit two stitches together; decreases one stitch

K1B: Knit 1 stitch in the row below (insert right needle into the stitch one row below the next stitch on the left needle).

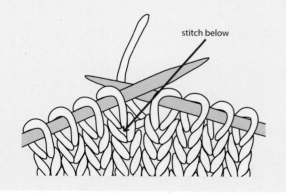

stitch below

INSTRUCTIONS

SCARF

With purple, cast on 25 stitches.

Rows 1 through 3: With purple, knit across.

Row 4: With purple, knit across. Attach white.

Row 5 (right side): With white, K3, *K1B, K1; repeat from * to last 2 stitches, K2.

Row 6 (wrong side): Knit across.

Row 7: With purple, K2, K1B, *K1, K1B; repeat from * to last 2 stitches, K2.

Row 8: Knit across.

Repeat Rows 5 through 8 until piece measures 72" from cast on row, ending by working Row 8. With purple, knit three rows. Bind off. Weave in all ends.

HAT

With purple, cast on 62 stitches.

Rows 1 and 2: With purple, knit across.

Row 3 (right side): With purple, *K1, K1B; repeat from * to last 2 stitches, K2.

Row 4 (wrong side): Knit across. Attach white.

Row 5: With white, K2, *K1B, K1; repeat from * across.

Row 6: With white, knit across.

Repeat Rows 3 through 6 until piece measures 6" from cast on row, ending with Row 6. Cut white and continue working with purple only.

Shape Crown

Row 1: With purple, *K1, KB; repeat from * to last 2 stitches, K2.

Rows 2, 3 and 4: Knit across.

Row 5: K3, *K6, K2tog; repeat from * to last 3 stitches, K3: 55 stitches.

Row 6: Knit across.

Row 7: K3, *K5, K2tog; repeat from * to last 3 stitches, K3: 48 stitches.

Row 8: Knit across.

Row 9: *K4, K2tog; repeat from * across: 40 stitches.

Row 10: Knit across.

Row 11: *K3, K2tog; repeat from * across: 32 stitches.

Row 12: Knit across.

Row 13: *K2, K2tog; repeat from * across: 24 stitches.

Row 14: Knit across.

Row 15: *K1, K2tog; repeat from * across: 16 stitches.

Rows 16 and 17: Knit across.

Cut yarn, leaving a long tail. Weave yarn through remaining 16 stitches and pull up tightly to secure. Join back seam, matching colors. Weave in all yarn ends.

Squares for Baby

Designed by Kathleen Sams for Red Heart®

The perfect project for the new knitter and the new mother, created simply in 36 squares joined together into a blanket to keep the new baby warm and comfy.

SKILL LEVEL

Beginner

SIZE

Approx 36" x 36" (91.44 cm x 91.44 cm)

MATERIALS

Light weight yarn

[80% acrylic, 20% nylon, 3.5 ounces, 340 yards (100 grams, 310 meters) per skein]

    2 skeins pink (A)

    2 skeins blue (B)

    2 skeins white (C)

Note: *Photographed model made with Red Heart® Anne Geddes Baby™ Rosie (A), Bluebell (B) and Lily (C)*

Size 6 (4 mm) knitting needles (or size required for gauge)

Yarn needle

GAUGE

22 stitches = 4" (10.16 cm) in garter stitch (knit each row)

INSTRUCTIONS

Pink Square (make 12)

With A, cast on 33 sts.

Row 1 (right side): Knit across.

Rows 2 through 64: Knit across.

Bind off. Weave in all ends.

Blue Square (make 12)

With B, cast on 33 sts.

Row 1 (right side): Knit across.

Rows 2 through 64: Knit across.

Bind off. Weave in all ends.

White Square (make 12)

With C, cast on 33 sts.

Row 1 (right side): Knit across.

Rows 2 through 64: Knit across.

Bind off. Weave in all ends. To assemble, lay pieces flat, join colors as indicated, or as you desire.

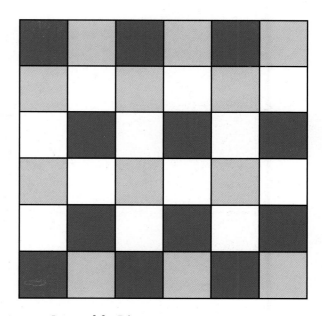

Assembly Diagram

Delightful Dishcloth

Add a note of color to the drab job of washing the dishes with an easy-to-make knitted dishcloth.

SKILL LEVEL

Easy

FINISHED SIZE

Approx 8" x 8" (20.32 cm x 20.32 cm)

MATERIALS

Worsted weight cotton yarn 〔4〕

[100% cotton, 2 ounces, 95 yards (57 grams, 86 meters) per ball]

    1 ball multi-color

Note: *Photographed model made with Lily® Sugar 'n Cream® #2600 Psychedelic*

Size 10 (6 mm) straight knitting needles (or size required for gauge)

GAUGE

8 sts = 2" (5.08 cm) in pattern

STITCH GUIDE

K: Knit

YO: yarn over a needle; creates one stitch.

K2tog: knit 2 stitches together; decreases one stitch.

INSTRUCTIONS

Cast on 2 stitches.

Increase Rows

Increase Row 1: Knit across.

Increase Row 2: K1, YO, K1: 3 stitches.

Increase Row 3: Knit across.

Increase Row 4: K1, (YO, K1) twice: 5 stitches.

Increase Row 5: Knit across.

Increase Row 6: K1, YO, knit across to last stitch, YO, K1: 7 sts.

Increase Row 7: Knit across.

Repeat Increase Row 6 and Increase Row 7 until there are 43 stitches on the needle.

Decrease Rows

Decrease Row 1: K1, YO, K2tog, knit across to last 3 stitches, K2tog, YO, K1: 43 stitches.

Decrease Row 2: K2, K2tog, knit across to last 4 stitches, K2tog, K2: 41 stitches.

Repeat Decrease Row 1 and Decrease Row 2 until there are 9 stitches on the needle.

Work the next 6 rows to complete the project.

Row 1: K1, YO, (K2tog) twice, K1; K2tog, YO, K1: 8 stitches.

Row 2: K2, (K2tog) twice, K2: 6 stitches.

Row 3: K1, YO, (K2tog) twice, YO, K1: 6 stitches.

Row 4: K1, (K2tog) twice, K1: 4 stitches.

Row 5: (K2tog) twice: 2 stitches.

Row 6: K2tog. Finish off; weave in all ends.

Lovely Lace

This lacy confection will be perfect for a bit of warmth on a summer evening.

SKILL LEVEL

Easy

FINIDHED SIZE

Approx 49" x 60" (124 cm x 152.40 cm)

MATERIALS

Worsted weight yarn

[100% acrylic, 7 ounces, 364 yards (198 grams, 333 meters) per skein]

    5 skeins white

Note: *Photographed model made with Red Heart® Super Saver® #316 Soft White.*

36" Size 10 (6 mm) circular knitting needle (or size required for gauge)

GAUGE

19 stitches = 4" (10.16 cm) in pattern

STITCH GUIDE

K: knit

P: purl

YO: yarn over a needle; creates one stitch

P3tog: purl 3 stitches together; decreases two stitches

INSTRUCTIONS

Cast on 234 stitches.

Note: *Do not join; work back and forth in rows.*

Rows 1 through 5: Knit across.

Row 6 (right side): Knit across.

Row 7: K4, Purl across to last 4 stitches, K4.

Row 8: K4; *K2, YO, P1, P3tog, P1, YO, repeat from * across to last 6 stitches; K6.

Row 9: K4, Purl across to last 4 stitches, K4.

Repeat Rows 6 through 9 until the piece measures approximately 59" (149.23 cm) from the cast-on row, ending by working Row 9.

Repeat Rows 1 through 5.

Finish off.

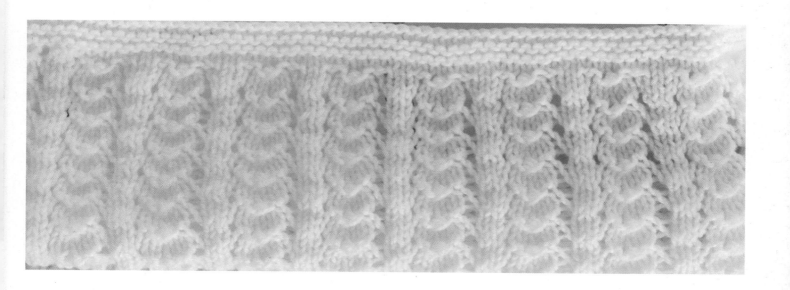

Sophisticated Cowl

Designed by Cathy Payson for Red Heart®

Lovely and dramatic, this cowl is quickly worked on large needles with two strands of yarn.

SKILL LEVEL

Easy

SIZE

Approx 11" x 32" (27.94 cm x 81.28 cm) before seaming

MATERIALS

Worsted weight yarn

[100% acrylic, 5 ounces, 236 yards (141 grams, 215 meters) per skein]

2 skeins multi-color

Note: *Photographed model made with Red Heart® Super Saver® #988 Platoon*

Size 13 (9 mm) knitting needles (or size required for gauge)

Yarn needle

GAUGE

11 stitches = 4" (10.16 cm) in pattern

STITCH GUIDE

K: knit

P: purl

Sl: slip the stitch from one needle to the next without working it

INSTRUCTIONS

Holding 2 strands of yarn together, loosely cast on 31 stitches.

Row 1 (wrong side): K1, purl across to last stitch, K1.

Row 2: K1; *sl 1 with yarn in back, K1; repeat from * across.

Repeat Rows 1 and 2 until piece measures approximately 32" (81.28 cm), ending by working a Row 1. Bind off all stitches loosely.

FINISHING

With yarn needle, sew cast on edge to bind off edge. Weave in all loose ends.

Warm Winter Hood and Scarf

This easy-to-knit hood is made extra long so that it offers double wrapping and double warmth to keep you cozy on the coldest days.

SKILL LEVEL

Beginner

SIZE

Approx 12" x 74" (30.48 cm x 187.96 cm)

MATERIALS

Worsted weight yarn 〔4〕

[100% acrylic, 3.5 ounces, 147 yards (100 grams, 134 meters) per skein]

    5 skeins self-striping yarn

Note: *Photographed model made with Lion Brand® Landscapes® #204 Desert Spring.*

Yarn needle

Size 10½ (6.5 mm) knitting needles (or size required for gauge)

GAUGE

12 sts = 3½" in garter stitch (knit each row)

INSTRUCTIONS

Cast on 42 stitches.

Row 1: Knit across.

Repeat Row 1 until piece measures 74" (187.96 cm). Finish off; weave in yarn ends.

Fold piece in half. Starting at fold, and using yarn needle, sew an 11" (27.94 cm) seam to form the hood.

Note: *For double warmth, place the hood over your head and wrap the scarf around your neck and back again. For casual wear, the front of the hood should be folded back and sewn in place.*

Four-Square Purse

A great purse to hold your knitting or your groceries, the color changes are automatically created by a clever yarn.

SKILL LEVEL

Easy

SIZE

Aprrox 16" x 16" (40.64 cm x 40.64 cm)

MATERIALS

Worsted weight yarn 4

[100% acrylic, 5 ounces, 224 yards (141 grams, 223 meters) per skein]

4 skeins black/grey

Note: *Photographed model made with Red Heart® Team Spirit™ #942 Black/Grey*

Size 5 (3.75 mm) knitting needles (or size required for gauge)

Two Size 5 (3.75 mm) double-pointed knitting needles

Yarn needle

GAUGE

20 stitches = 4" (10.16 cm) in garter stitch (knit each row)

INSTRUCTIONS

Purse Front

Square (make 4)

Cast on 40 sts.

Row 1: Knit across.

Repeat Row 1 until each piece measures 8" and is a perfect square.

Bind off all stitches. Weave in all yarn ends.

Assembly

Sew two pairs of two squares together, joining the cast-on edge to a side edge as shown in the photo. Then sew the two sets together, again making certain that the cast-on edges are sewn to the side edges.

Purse Back

Repeat Purse Front directions.

Finishing

With right sides together, join the Purse Back to the Purse Front. Sew the sides and bottom edge. Turn purse inside out.

STRAPS (make two)

Note: *Cords are worked from the right side only; do not turn. Stitches will fold toward the wrong side to form a double thickness cord.*

With 2 strands of yarn, cast on 3 stitches on one double-pointed knitting needle.

Row 1: With second double-pointed knitting needle, knit 3; do not turn. Slide stitches to opposite end of the needle.

Row 2: Take yarn around the back side of the stitches and with 2nd needle, knit 3; do not turn. Slide the stitches to the opposite end of the needle.

Repeat Rows 1 and 2 until the cord is the desired length. Bind off.

Wristers

Designed by Darla Sims for Red Heart®

Keep your hands warm while your fingers do fun things, like knitting. Make them for your friends in your school colors and cheer your team at the next game.

SKILL LEVEL

Easy

FINISHED SIZE

Approx 8" (20.32 cm) long and 8" (20.32 cm) circumference

MATERIALS

Worsted weight yarn

[100% acrylic, 5 ounces, 244 yards (141 grams, 223 meters) per skein]

    1 skein red/blue

Note: *Photographed model made with Red Heart® Team Spirit™ #940 Red/Blue.*

Size 9 (5.5 mm) knitting needles (or size required for gauge)

Yarn needle

GAUGE

15 stitches = 4" (10.16 cm) in stockinette stitch (knit 1 row; purl 1 row)

STITCH GUIDE

K: knit

P: purl

INSTRUCTIONS (make 2)

Cuff

Cast on 34 stitches.

Row 1 (right side): K2, *P2, K2; repeat from * across.

Row 2: P2, *K2, P2 across; repeat from * across.

Repeat Rows 1 and 2 for Cuff until piece measures approximately 2" (5.08 cm) from cast on edge, ending by working a Row 2.

Body

Row 1 (right side): Knit across.

Row 2: Purl across.

Repeat Rows 1 and 2 for body until the piece measures approximately 7" (17.78 cm) from the cast on edge, ending with Row 2.

Thumb Opening

Row 1 (right side): K27, bind off next 5 stitches, Knit across remaining stitches: 29 stitches.

Row 2: P2, cast on 5 stitches, purl across remaining stitches: 34 stitches.

Hand

Row 1 (right side): K2, *P2, K2; repeat from * across.

Row 2: P2, *K2, P2; repeat from * across.

Repeat Rows 1 and 2 for Hand until piece measures approximately 8" (20.32 cm) from the cast on edge, ending by working Row 2.

Bind off all stitches in pattern. Cut the yarn, leaving a long end for sewing.

Finishing

Thread the yarn needle with the long end. With right sides together and matching stitches, sew the seam.

Tablet Cozy

Protect your precious electronic tablet from dings and scratches by knitting a special cover that's quick and easy to create.

SKILL LEVEL

Beginner

FINISHED SIZE

Approx 10½" x 7" (26.67 cm x 45.72 cm)

MATERIALS

Worsted weight yarn

[100% acrylic, 5 ounces, 266 yards (141 grams, 243 meters) per skein]

　　1 skein brown tweed

Note: *Photographed model made with Red Heart® Super Tweed® #7901 Fire*

Size 8 (5 mm) knitting needles (or size required for gauge)

Yarn needle

GAUGE

16 sts = 4" (10.16 cm) in garter stitch (knit every row)

STITCH GUIDE

K: knit

P: purl

INSTRUCTIONS

Cast on 32 stitches.

Border One

Row 1: *K2, P2; repeat from * across.

Repeat Row 1 of Border One until piece measures 1½" (3.81 cm).

Body

Row 1: Knit across.

Repeat Row 1 of Body until piece measures 19½" (49.53 cm).

Border Two

Row 1: *K2, P2; repeat from * across.

Repeat Row 1 of Border Two until both borders are the same size, and the total piece measures 21" (53.34 cm).

FINISHING

Bind off all stitches. With right sides facing, fold the knitting in half from top to bottom, meeting the two borders. Sew both long seams. Weave in all ends. Turn right side out.

Phone Cozies

Protect and personalize your cell phone by knitting this quick and easy cover.

SKILL LEVEL

Easy

FINISHED SIZES

6" long x 3" wide (15.24 cm x 7.62 cm)

6½" long x 3" wide (16.51 cm x 7.62 cm)

MATERIALS

Worsted weight yarn

[100% acrylic, 5 ounces, 266 yards (141 grams, 243 meters) per skein]

　　1 skein brown tweed

Note: *Photographed model made with Red Heart® Super Tweed® #7901 Fire*

Size 8 (5 mm) knitting needles (or size required for gauge)

Yarn needle

GAUGE

16 sts = 4" (10.16 cm) in garter stitch (knit every row)

STITCH GUIDE

K: knit

P: purl

INSTRUCTIONS

Note: *Instructions are written for the smaller size, with instructions for the larger size in parentheses.*

Cast on 14 sts (16 sts).

FIRST BORDER

Row 1: *K2, P2; repeat from * across the row.

Repeat Row 1 of Border until piece measures 1" (1").

BODY

Row 1: Knit across.

Repeat Row 1 of body until piece measures 11" (12½)".

SECOND BORDER

Row 1: *K2, P2; repeat from * across the row,

Repeat Row 1 of Border until both Borders are the same size and the piece measures 12" (13½") total.

Bind off stitches loosely across.

Using yarn needle and yarn, fold cozy in half with right sides facing. Sew each side seam evenly. Turn right side out.

Raspberries and Cream

*Red and creamy white yarns are beautifully combined for a fresh look
that's almost good enough to eat!*

SKILL LEVEL

Easy ◼◼☐☐

FINISHED SIZE

Approx 40" x 60" (101.60 cm x 152.40 cm)

MATERIALS

Worsted weight yarn

[100% acrylic, 7 ounces, 364 yards (198 grams, 333 meters) per skein]

    3 skeins red (A)

    1 skein white (B)

Note: *Photographed model made with Red Heart® Super Saver® #3901 Rouge (A) and #313 Aran (B)*

29" Size 8 (5 mm) circular knitting needle (or size required for gauge)

GAUGE

16 stitches = 4" (10.16 cm) in pattern

STITCH GUIDE

K: knit

P: purl

K2tog: knit 2 stitches together; decreases one stitch

YO: yarn over needle; creates one stitch

SI: slip stitch from one needle to the next without working it

PSSO: pass the slip stitch over the knit stitch

INSTRUCTIONS

With white, cast on 165 stitches.

Note: *Do not join; work back and forth in rows.*

Rows 1 through 4: Knit across. Cut white; attach red.

Row 5: With red, K5; *(K2tog) twice, (YO, K1) 3 times, YO; (SI 1, K1, PSSO) twice, K1; repeat from * across to last 4 stitches, K4.

Row 6: K4, purl across to the last 4 stitches, K4.

Row 7: Repeat Row 5.

Row 8: Repeat Row 6.

Row 9: Repeat Row 5.

Row 10: Repeat Row 6.

Row 11: Repeat Row 5.

Row 12: Repeat Row 6.

Row 13: Repeat Row 5.

Row 14: Repeat Row 6.

Row 15: Repeat Row 5.

Row 16: Repeat Row 6. At end of Row 16, cut red and attach white.

Rows 17 through 20: With white, knit across. At end of Row 20, cut white and attach red.

Repeat Rows 5 through 20 of pattern until the piece measures 60" (152.40 cm) from beginning, ending by working Row 20.

Bind off loosely as to knit.

Fabulous Face Cloth

Add a little joy to your cleaning routine with original knitted face cloths.

SKILL LEVEL

Easy ◖■▢▭

FINISHED SIZE

Approx 10" x 10" (25.40 cm x 25.40 cm)

MATERIALS

Worsted weight cotton yarn (4)

[100% cotton, 2 ½ ounces, 120 yards (71 grams, 109 meters) per ball]

    1 ball green

Note: *Photographed model made with Lily® Sugar 'n Cream® #084 Sage Green*

Size 7 (4.5 mm) knitting needles

GAUGE

10 sts = 2" (5.08 cm) in garter stitch (knit each row)

STITCH GUIDE

K: knit

YO: yarn over a needle; creates one stitch

K2tog: knit 2 stitches together; decreases one stitch

INSTRUCTIONS

Cast on 4 stitches.

Row 1: Knit across.

Row 2: Knit in the front and back of each stitch: 8 stitches.

Row 3: Knit across.

Row 4: K4, YO, knit across to the end of the row: 9 stitches.

Rows 5 through 49: Repeat Row 4. At the end of Row 49: 54 stitches.

Rows 50 and 51: K4, YO, K2tog; knit across to the end of the row.

Row 52: K3, K2tog, YO, K2tog; knit across to the end of the row.

Rows 53 through 96: Repeat Row 52. At the end of Row 96: 9 stitches.

Row 97: K3, K2tog, K4: 8 stitches.

Row 98: K8.

Row 99: (K2tog) 4 times: 4 stitches.

Finish off. Weave in ends.

Lapghan

Designed by Marilyn Coleman for Red Heart®

When a big afghan would be too clumsy in your small chair, why not scare the chills away with this perfect-sized lapghan.

SKILL LEVEL

Easy

FINISHED SIZE

Approx 37½" x 37½"
(95.25 cm x 95.25 cm)

MATERIALS

Worsted weight yarn 4
[100% acrylic, 7 ounces,
364 yards (198 grams,
333 meters) per skein]

  1 skein off white (A)

  1 skein light blue (B)

  1 skein dark blue (C)

Note: *Photographed model made with Red Heart® Super Saver® #313 Aran (A), #382 Country Blue (B) and #387 Soft Navy (C)*

Size 8 (5 mm) knitting needles (or size required for gauge)

Yarn needle

GAUGE

17 sts = 4" (10.16 cm) in pattern

STITCH GUIDE

K: knit

P: purl

INSTRUCTIONS

Strips 1 and 4

With A, cast on 33 sts.

Row 1 (right side): Knit across.

Row 2: P1, *K1, P1; repeat from * across.

Repeat Rows 1 and 2 for the pattern until the piece measures 7½" (19.05 cm) from the cast on edge, ending by working Row 2. Cut A and attach B.

With B, repeat Rows 1 and 2 for the pattern until the piece now measures 15" (38.10 cm) from the cast on edge, ending by working Row 2. Cut B and attach C.

With C, repeat Rows 1 and 2 for the pattern until the piece measures 22½" (57.15 cm) from the cast on edge, ending by working Row 2. Cut C and attach A.

With A, repeat Rows 1 and 2 for pattern until piece measures 30" (76.20 cm) from cast on edge, ending by working Row 2. Cut A and attach B.

With B, repeat Rows 1 and 2 for pattern until piece measures 37½" (95.25 cm) from cast on edge, ending by working Row 2. Bind off all stitches.

Strips 2 and 5

With B, cast on 33 stitches.

Row 1 (right side): Knit across.

Row 2: P1, *K1, P1; repeat from * across.

Repeat Rows 1 and 2 for the pattern until the piece now measures 7½" (19.05 cm) from the cast on edge, ending by working Row 2. Cut B and attach C.

With C, repeat Rows 1 and 2 for the pattern until the piece measures 15" (38.10 cm) from the cast on edge, ending by working Row 2. Cut C and attach A.

With A, repeat Rows 1 and 2 for pattern until piece measures 22½" (57.15 cm) from cast on edge, ending by working Row 2. Cut A and attach B.

With B, repeat Rows 1 and 2 for pattern until piece measures 30" (76.20 cm) from cast on edge, ending by working Row 2. Cut B and attach C.

With C, repeat Rows 1 and 2 for the pattern until the piece measures 37½" (95.25 cm) from the cast on edge, ending by working Row 2. Bind off all stitches.

Strip 3

With C, cast on 33 stitches.

Row 1 (right side): Knit across.

Row 2: P1, *K1, P1; repeat from * across.

Repeat Rows 1 and 2 for the pattern until the piece now measures 7½" (19.05 cm) from the cast on edge, ending by working Row 2. Cut C and attach A.

With A, repeat Rows 1 and 2 for the pattern until the piece measures 15" (38.10 cm) from the cast on edge, ending by working Row 2. Cut A and attach B.

With B, repeat Rows 1 and 2 for pattern until piece measures 22½" (57.15 cm) from cast on edge, ending by working Row 2. Cut B and attach C.

With C, repeat Rows 1 and 2 for pattern until piece measures 30" (76.20 cm) from cast on edge, ending by working Row 2. Cut C and attach A.

With A, repeat Rows 1 and 2 for the pattern until the piece measures 37½" (95.25 cm) from the cast on edge, ending by working Row 2. Bind off all stitches.

FINISHING

Thread yarn needle with desired color. With right sides together, using **chart** below as a guide and matching rows, sew strips together in numerical order.

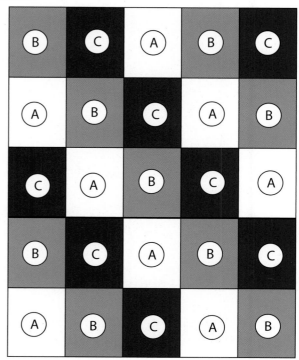

A Little Bit of Fur

Just a small fur scarf is all you need to add the perfect touch? Then just use this yarn and your knitting needles to create your very own fur scarf…and not an animal was harmed.

SKILL LEVEL

Easy

FINISHED SIZE

Approx 6" x 58" (17.78 cm x 147.32 cm)

MATERIALS

Bulky weight yarn (5)

[100% Polyester, 1.75 ounces, 64 yards (50 grams, 58 meters) per skein]

3 skeins beige

Note: *Photographed model made with Lion Brand® Fun Fur® #124 Champagne*

Size 10½ (6.5 mm) knitting needles (or size required for gauge)

GAUGE

9 stitches = 2" (5.08 cm) in pattern

STITCH GUIDE

K: knit

P: purl

INSTRUCTIONS

Cast on 27 stitches loosely.

Rows 1 through 5: Knit across.

Row 6 (wrong side): K2, P23, K2.

Row 7 (right side): Knit across.

Repeat Rows 6 and 7 until the piece measures 57" from the cast on row, ending by working a right side row.

Knit 4 rows. Bind off and weave in all ends.

Coffee Cup Cozy

Designed by Grace Alexander for Red Heart®

The perfect gift for the coffee or tea drinker. Keep a few handy in the car so hot drinks will be easy to handle on the way to work.

SKILL LEVEL

Beginner ◖☐☐☐

FINISHED SIZE

Approx 3" (7.62 cm) deep; fits most paper coffee cups

MATERIALS

Worsted weight yarn

[100% acrylic, 7 ounces, 370 yards (198 grams, 338 meters) per skein]

    1 skein purple

Note: *Photographed model made with Red Heart® Super Saver® #356 Amethyst*

Size 7 (4.5 mm) knitting needles (or size required for gauge)

Yarn needle

GAUGE

18 sts = 4" (10.16 cm) in stockinette stitch (knit 1 row, purl 1 row)

STITCH GUIDE

K: knit

P: purl

K2tog: knit 2 stitches together; decreases one stitch

INSTRUCTIONS

Body

Cast on 39 stitches.

Row 1 (right side): K1, *P1, K1; repeat from * across.

Row 2 (wrong side): K1, *P1, K1; repeat from * across.

Repeat Rows 1 and 2 until the piece measures 2" (5.08 cm) from the beginning, ending by working a wrong-side row. Do not end off. Continue with Cuff.

Cuff

Row 1 (right side): K2tog, P1, *K1, P1; repeat from * across: 38 stitches.

Row 2: *K1, P1; repeat from * across.

Repeat Row 2 until the piece measures 3" (7.62 cm) from the beginning, ending with a wrong-side row.

Bind off in pattern.

Sew the seam with yarn needle; weave in all ends.

Saucy But Sweet Hat and Scarf

What "tween" wouldn't love wearing this sassy hat and matching scarf!

SKILL LEVEL

Easy ◧☐☐☐◗

FINISHED SIZE

Scarf: Approx 12" x 72" (30.48 cm x 182.88 cm)

Hat: Approx 16" to 18" (40.64 cm to 45.72 cm) circumference

MATERIALS

Bulky weight yarn

[80% acrylic, 20% wool, 3.5 ounces, 106 yards (100 grams, 97 meters) per skein]

Hat: 1 skein navy, 1 skein white

Scarf: 3 skeins navy, 3 skeins white

Note: *Photographed model made with Red Heart® Heads Up™ #852 Navy and #100 Ivory.*

Scarf: Size 13 (9 mm) knitting needles (or size equired for gauge)

Hat: Size 11 (8 mm) knitting needles (or size equired for gauge)

Large-eye blunt yarn needle

GAUGE

Scarf

12 sts = 4" (10.16 cm) in garter stitch (knit each row)

Hat

14 sts = 4" (10.16 cm) in garter stitch (knit each row)

INSTRUCTIONS

SCARF

With navy yarn and size 13 needles, cast on 36 stitches.

Row 1 (right side): Knit across.

Rows 2 through 6: Knit across each row. At the end of Row 6, cut the navy yarn, and attach the white yarn, leaving long enough ends for weaving in at the end.

Rows 7 through 12: With white, knit across each row. At the end of Row 12, cut the white yarn and attach the navy yarn.

Repeat Rows 1 through 12 twenty-five additional times, ending last six rows with navy.

Bind off. Weave in all yarn ends.

HAT

With navy and size 11 needles, cast on 28 stitches loosely.

Rows 1 through 6 : Knit across each row. At the end of Row 6, cut the navy yarn, and attach the white yarn, leaving long enough ends for weaving in at the end.

Rows 7 through 12: With white, knit across each row. At the end of Row 12, cut the white yarn and attach the navy yarn.

Repeat this 12-row striping pattern until you have alternating 5 stripes of navy with 5 stripes of white, ending with a white stripe. Cut white and attach navy.

Next 12 rows: Using navy, knit all 12 rows. (This is the crown of the hat, where it will fold when sewing up the sides.) Cut navy and attach white.

Next 6 rows: Using white, knit all 6 rows. Cut white and attach navy.

Next 6 rows: Using navy, knit all 6 rows.

Repeat this 12-row striping pattern until you have alternating 5 stripes of white with 5 stripes of navy, ending with a navy stripe.

Next Row: Bind off all stitches across loosely.

Finishing

Fold hat at the middle of the wide blue stripe with right sides together. Carefully matching stripes, sew side seams, starting at the bottom and continuing to the top.

Turn hat right side out and flip up brim.

A Family of Hats

Knit a pair of matching hats for both mother and her daughter!

FINISHED SIZE

Daughter: 17¾" (45.09 cm) circumference

Mother: 20" (50.8 cm) circumference

MATERIALS

Worsted weight yarn 4

[100% acrylic, 7 ounces, 370 yards (198 grams, 338 meters) per skein]

   1 skein light pink (daughter)

   1 skein pink (mother)

Note: *Photographed model made with Red Heart® With Love® #1704 Bubblegum (daughter) and #1701 Hot Pink (mother).*

Size 9 (5.5 mm) knitting needles (or size required for gauge)

Yarn needle

GAUGE

14 stitches = 4" (10.16 cm) in K2, P2 ribbing

STITCH GUIDE

K: knit

P: purl

K2tog: knit 2 stitches together; decreases one stitch

SSK: slip next two stitches as if to knit, one at a time, to right needle; insert the tip of the left needle into the front of these two stitches and knit these two stitches together through the back loop; decreases one stitch.

DAUGHTER'S HAT INSTRUCTIONS

Cuff

Cast on 62 stitches.

Row 1 (right side): *K2, P2; repeat from * across the row.

Row 2: *P2, K2; repeat from * across the row.

Continue to work Rows 1 and 2 until the piece measures approximately 5" (12.7 cm) from the cast on edge, ending by working a wrong side row.

Body

Row 1 (right side): Knit across.

Row 2: Purl across.

Continue to work Rows 1 and 2 until the piece measures approximately 8" (20.32 cm) from cast on edge, ending by working a wrong side row.

Crown Shaping

Row 1 (right side): K1, *K2 tog, K11, SSK; repeat from * across to the last stitch, K1: 54 stitches.

Row 2: Purl across.

Row 3: K1, *K2tog, K9, SSK; repeat from * across to the last stitch, K1: 46 stitches.

Row 4: Purl across.

Row 5: K1, *K2tog, K7, SSK; repeat from * across to the last stitch, K1: 38 stitches.

Row 6: Purl across.

Row 7: K1, *K2tog, K5, SSK; repeat from * across to the last stitch, K1: 30 stitches.

Row 8: Purl across.

Row 9: K1, *K2tog, K3, SSK; repeat from * across to the last stitch, K1: 22 stitches.

Row 10: Purl across.

Row 11: K1, *K2tog, K1, SSK; repeat from * across to the last stitch, K1: 14 stitches.

Row 12: Purl across.

Cut the yarn, leaving a 16" (40.6 cm) end. Thread the yarn needle with the end and weave it through the remaining stitches; draw up firmly; fasten securely.

Finishing

With right sides together and matching stitches, sew seam. Following the instructions on page 46, make a pompon and attach it securely to hat.

MOTHER'S HAT INSTRUCTIONS

Cuff

Cast on 70 stitches.

Row 1 (right side): *K2, P2; repeat from * across the row.

Row 2: *P2, K2; repeat from * across the row.

Continue to work Rows 1 and 2 until the piece measures approximately 6" (15.24 cm) from the cast on edge, ending by working a wrong side row.

Instructions continued on page 46

Body

Row 1 (right side): Knit across.

Row 2: Purl across.

Continue to work Rows 1 and 2 until the piece measures approximately 9" (22.86 cm) from cast on edge, ending by working a wrong side row.

Crown Shaping

Row 1 (right side): K1, *K2 tog, K13, SSK; repeat from * across to the last stitch, K1: 62 stitches.

Row 2: Purl across.

Row 3: K1, *K2tog, K11, SSK; repeat from * across to the last stitch, K1: 54 stitches.

Row 4: Purl across.

Row 5: K1, *K2tog, K9, SSK; repeat from * across to the last stitch, K1: 46 stitches.

Row 6: Purl across.

Row 7: K1, *K2tog, K7, SSK; repeat from * across to the last stitch, K1: 38 stitches.

Row 8: Purl across.

Row 9: K1, *K2tog, K5, SSK; repeat from * across to the last stitch, K1: 30 stitches.

Row 10: Purl across.

Row 11: K1, *K2tog, K3, SSK; repeat from * across to the last stitch, K1: 22 stitches.

Row 12: Purl across.

Row 13: K1, *K2tog, K1, SSK; repeat from * across to last st, K1: 44 sts.

Row 14: Purl across.

Cut the yarn, leaving a 16" (40.6 cm) end. Thread the yarn needle with the end and weave it through the remaining stitches; draw up firmly; fasten securely.

Finishing

With right sides together and matching stitches, sew seam. Following the instructions below, make a pompon, and attach it securely to the hat.

Pompons

From cardboard, cut two circles ½" larger in diameter than desired size of the pompon. In the center of each circle, cut or punch a ½" hole. Hold the two circles together and thread two long strands of yarn into a yarn needle. Going from the outer edge to the center of the circles, wrap the yarn around the circles until they are full, adding new yarn as needed. With sharp scissors, cut yarn around the outer edge of the circles. Cut a piece of yarn 6" long and insert between the circles. Draw up tightly and knot. Remove cardboard circles. Rub the pompon in your palms to fluff; trim to desired size.

STITCH GUIDE

Knit 2 stitches together (K2tog)

Insert the needle from left to right through the fronts of 2 stitches on the left needle and bring the yarn under and over the point of the needle.

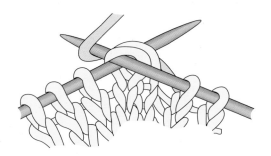

Draw the yarn through both stitches. Slip both stitches off the left needle, and one new stitch will be on the right needle. One stitch has been decreased.

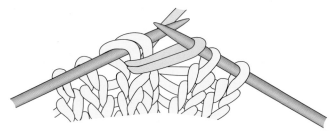

Purl 2 stitches together (P2tog)
Purl 3 stitches together (P3tog)

In much the same way, you can purl 2 or 3 stitches together. Insert the right-hand needle from right to left through the fronts of 2 purl stitches on the left needle. Wrap the working thread around as if you were purling one stitch.

Slip (sl)

Slip the stitch from one needle to the other without working it. Insert the right needle into the stitch as if to purl (even if it is a knit stitch), but instead of actually purling, slip the stitch from the left needle to the right needle.

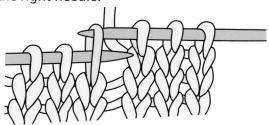

Yarn Over (YO)

Used to make an increase, the Yarn Over is basically just a loop of yarn that goes over the top of the working needle, moving first in front of the needle and then down in the back.

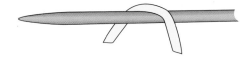

The stitch always begins with the yarn in front of the needle. For making a YO after a knit stitch, bring the yarn forward as if to purl, wrap the yarn over the needle and knit the next stitch.

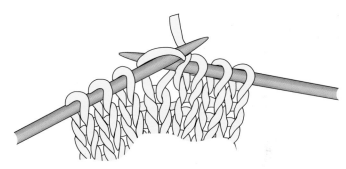

A YO can be made after a purl stitch as well. Since the yarn will be in the correct spot in front of the needle, just take the yarn over the top of the right needle and then bring it between the two needles to the front again. The needle will once again be in the correct position to purl the next stitch.

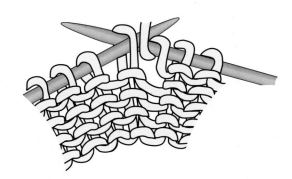

47

Instructions continued on page 48

Slip, Slip, Knit (SSK)

At place where decrease is to be made, slip next two stitches, one at a time, as if to knit, to the right needle.

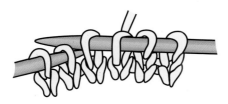

Insert left needle into fronts of these two stitches and knit them together.

Pass the Slipped Stitch Over (PSSO)

Insert right needle, as if to knit, into the stitch, slip this stitch onto right-hand needle without knitting it, then knit the next stitch.

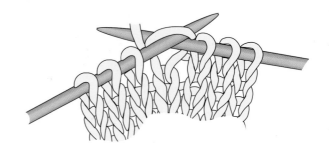

Using the left-hand needle, lift slipped stitch over the knit stitch and off the needle.

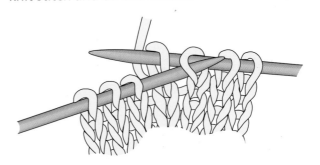

Special Helps

Attaching new yarn

At the end of a row, tie the new color yarn around the old color yarn, making a knot at the end of the project. Leave a 4" end on both the new and the old color. Cut off the old color. Work with the new color. When the work is finished, untie the knots and weave in all of the ends.

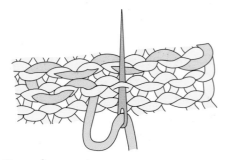

Weaving in the ends

Thread the yarn needle with a yarn end and weave it through the backs of the stitches. Weave about 2" in one direction and then about 1" in the opposite direction. Carefully trim off any extra yarn. Never permit the needle to go through to the front of the work.

Sewing seams

Cut an 18" piece of matching yarn and thread it into the needle. With right sides of pieces facing each other and the stitches placed even in a row, insert the needle from the back to the front through the strands at the edges of the pieces between the stitches. Pull the yarn end gently but firmly. The two pieces will come together. Weave in all loose ends.

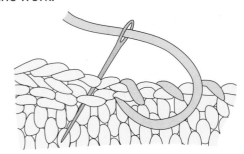